BRUNCH
COCKTAILS

13-Digit ISBN: 978-0-31016-783-9
10-Digit ISBN: 0-31016-783-3

This book may be ordered by mail from the publisher. Please include $5.99 for postage and handling. Please support your local bookseller first!

Books published by Cider Mill Press Book Publishers are available at special discounts for bulk purchases in the United States by corporations, institutions, and other organizations. For more information, please contact the publisher.

Cider Mill Press Book Publishers
"Where good books are ready for press"
501 Nelson Place
Nashville, Tennessee 37214
cidermillpress.com

Typography: New Frank, Trade Gothic Next LT

Image Credits: Pages 4–5, 28, 48, 51, 52, 57, 58, 61, 62, 65, 67, 68, 71, 72, 77, 78, 81, 82–83, 84–85, 86, 89, 90, 93, 94, 100–101, 102, 104–105, 107, 108–109, 110–111, 112, 115, 116, 119, 120, 123, 124, 127, 128, 130, 132, 135, 136, 139, 140, 142–143, 144, 147, 150, 153, 154, 156–157, 160, 163, 164, 167, 168, 171, 172, 175, 176, 179, 180, 183, 186–187, 189, 190, and 193 courtesy of Cider Mill Press. Pages 6, 10, 14, 19, 20, 23, 39, and 40 courtesy of Unsplash. All other photos used under official license from Shutterstock.

Printed in Malaysia

24 25 26 27 28 OFF 5 4 3 2 1

First Edition

BRUNCH
COCKTAILS

**THE ART
OF BOOZY
BRUNCHES
& DAYTIME
DRINKING**

y

CIDER MILL
PRESS

BOOK
PUBLISHERS

CONTENTS

INTRODUCTION

The weekend has finally arrived and you're ready to make the most of it.

After a leisurely morning, you think to yourself, "How do I make this a weekend to remember?" From all corners of your mind, the response resounds: "Brunch!"

You immediately assent, blow past the brief alarm that sounds when you recognize that you don't have a resy, contact a few friends, and head out the door.

Turning the corner, you see gaggle of people waiting in various grim poses. "Maybe they're just waiting for takeout," you think. "A latte." And so continue to the host stand, where the host stands, furiously scribbling at something, exasperation radiating off of them.

After a beat, they look up.

"How long?" You ask.

"Two hours, maybe more," comes the inhospitable response.

Do you stick to the plan, wait and watch the day slip away, or head home and try to recover from this abrupt letdown? Whichever way you go, the glorious beginning you'd charted just 30 minutes ago will be torn to shreds.

Somehow, instead of a triumphant weekend, you've backed yourself into a no-win situation.

We've all been there.

Luckily, there's a solution—hosting brunch at home. If you can crack an egg and stir a drink, it's by far the best way to ensure that your weekends start off with the bang you deserve, propelling you into a series of occasions that you look back on with fondness decades later.

To encourage this development, we've collected the very best brunch cocktail recipes to make your job as host much easier. With these in hand, you'll be able to strike the perfect tone for each and every occasion, rise to meet each and every request, and transform brunch from a source of disappointment to a can't-miss event that supplies the energy and joy you need in order to face the week ahead.

CLASSICS

As a veteran of numerous brunches, each and every one of these drinks will look familiar to you. That is not to say that they are worn out, however. They have stood the test of time for a reason, and will serve you well when you start to host your own brunches. Get each and every one down and then explore the vast space for experimentation that surrounds them. Once you make these your own, your weekend brunches will become standing appointments for your friends and loved ones.

IRISH COFFEE

GLASSWARE: Irish coffee glass
GARNISH: Whipped cream (optional)

---

3 oz. freshly brewed coffee
Dash of sugar
1 oz. Irish whiskey
1 oz. Irish cream liqueur

---

1. Pour the coffee into the Irish coffee glass, add the sugar, and stir until the sugar has dissolved.

2. Stir in the whiskey and liqueur. Garnish with whipped cream (if desired) and enjoy.

FRENCH 75

GLASSWARE: Champagne flute
GARNISH: Lemon twist, maraschino cherry

---

1 sugar cube
Juice of 1 lemon wedge
1 oz. gin
2 oz. Champagne
1 lemon twist, for garnish
1 maraschino cherry, for garnish

---

1. Place the sugar cube in the Champagne flute and add the lemon juice.

2. Add the gin and top with the Champagne.

3. Garnish the cocktail with the lemon twist. Skewer the cherry with a toothpick and place it over the mouth of the champagne flute.

GLASSWARE: Wineglass
GARNISH: Orange slice

---

3 oz. prosecco
2 oz. Aperol
1 oz. seltzer

---

1. Fill the wineglass with ice and add the ingredients in the order they are listed.

2. Gently lift the Aperol with a bar spoon, garnish with the orange slice, and enjoy.

APEROL SPRITZ

PALOMA

GLASSWARE: Collins glass
GARNISH: Grapefruit wedge, fresh rosemary

Salt, for the rim
2 oz. tequila
1 oz. grapefruit juice
½ oz. fresh lime juice
Pink grapefruit soda, to top

---

1. Wet the rim of the Collins glass and rim it with salt.

2. Fill the Collins glass with ice, add the tequila, grapefruit juice, and lime juice, and stir until chilled.

3. Top with grapefruit soda, gently stir, garnish with the grapefruit wedge and fresh rosemary, and enjoy.

TEQUILA SUNRISE

GLASSWARE: Collins glass
GARNISH: Maraschino cherry, orange slice

---

2 oz. tequila
Dash of fresh lemon juice
4 oz. orange juice
Splash of grenadine

---

1. Fill the Collins glass with ice, add the tequila, lemon juice, and orange juice, and stir until chilled.

2. Add the grenadine and do not stir, letting it slowly filter down through the orange juice.

3. Garnish with the maraschino cherry and orange slice and enjoy.

ESPRESSO MARTINI

GLASSWARE: Cocktail glass
GARNISH: 3 espresso beans

2 oz. vodka

1 oz. freshly brewed espresso

½ oz. coffee liqueur

1. Chill the cocktail glass in the freezer.

2. Place all of the ingredients in a cocktail shaker, fill it two-thirds of the way with ice, and shake until chilled.

3. Double strain into the chilled glass and garnish with the espresso beans.

SCREWDRIVER

GLASSWARE: Collins glass
GARNISH: Orange slice

---

2 oz. vodka
4 oz. orange juice

---

1. Fill the Collins glass with ice, add the vodka, and top with the orange juice.

2. Stir until chilled and garnish with the orange slice.

BLOODY MARY

GLASSWARE: Pint glass
GARNISH: Anything your heart desires

---

4 dashes of salt

2 dashes of cayenne pepper

2 dashes of ground black pepper

6 dashes of Worcestershire sauce

Juice of ½ lemon

2 oz. vodka

2 oz. tomato juice

---

1. Fill the pint glass with ice, add all of the ingredients, and stir until chilled.

2. Garnish with anything your heart desires. Celery, olives, bacon, lemon wedges, and pickles are popular options.

MIMOSA

GLASSWARE: Champagne flute
GARNISH: None

---

3 oz. orange juice
3 oz. Champagne

---

1. Place the orange juice in the Champagne flute, top with the Champagne, and enjoy.

GLASSWARE: Champagne coupe
GARNISH: None

---

2 oz. peach nectar
¼ oz. fresh lemon juice
Champagne, to top

---

1. Place the peach nectar and lemon juice in a cocktail shaker, fill it two-thirds of the way with ice, and shake until chilled.

2. Strain into the champagne coupe, top with Champagne, and enjoy.

BELLINI

BREAKFAST MARTINI

GLASSWARE: Cocktail glass
GARNISH: Orange twist

1¾ oz. gin
1 bar spoon orange marmalade
½ oz. Cointreau
½ oz. fresh lemon juice

---

1. Place the gin and marmalade in a cocktail shaker and stir until well combined.

2. Add ice and the remaining ingredients and shake until chilled.

3. Strain into the cocktail glass and garnish with the orange twist.

PIMM'S CUP

GLASSWARE: Collins glass
GARNISH: Fresh mint

---

1 oz. Pimm's No. 1
1 orange slice
1 lemon slice
1 cucumber slice
1 strawberry, hulled and sliced
2 oz. lemonade
2½ oz. ginger ale

---

1. Add ice to the Collins glass, pour in the Pimm's, and stir until chilled.

2. Add the orange, lemon, cucumber, and strawberry, top with the lemonade and ginger ale, and gently stir.

3. Garnish with fresh mint and enjoy.

PIMM'S CUP

See page 31

GLASSWARE: Coupe
GARNISH: Freshly grated nutmeg

---

3 oz. whole milk

1 oz. half & half

2 oz. brandy

1 oz. Simple Syrup (see recipe)

½ teaspoon pure vanilla extract

---

1. Chill the coupe in the freezer.

2. Place all of the ingredients in a cocktail shaker, fill it two-thirds of the way with ice, and shake until chilled.

3. Strain into the chilled coupe, garnish with nutmeg, and enjoy.

SIMPLE SYRUP: Place 1 cup sugar and 1 cup water in a saucepan and bring it to a boil, stirring to dissolve the sugar. Remove the pan from heat and let the syrup cool completely before using or storing.

BRANDY MILK PUNCH

PAINKILLER

GLASSWARE: Mug or mason jar
GARNISH: Freshly grated nutmeg, orange slice

---

2 oz. navy rum (Pusser's recommended)
1 oz. cream of coconut
1 oz. orange juice
4 oz. pineapple juice

---

1. Place all of the ingredients in a cocktail shaker, fill it two-thirds of the way with crushed ice, and shake until chilled.

2. Pour the contents of the shaker into a mug or mason jar, garnish with nutmeg and the orange slice, and enjoy.

GLASSWARE: Wineglass
GARNISH: None

---

1 oz. absinthe
½ oz. Herbsaint
½ oz. crème de menthe
1 oz. heavy cream
¼ oz. Simple Syrup (see page 35)
Dash of orange blossom water
1 egg white

---

1. Chill the wineglass in the freezer.

2. Place all of the ingredients in a cocktail shaker and dry shake for 15 seconds.

3. Add ice and shake until chilled.

4. Strain into the chilled wineglass and enjoy.

ABSINTHE SUISSESSE

SANGRIA

1 (750 ml) bottle of dry red wine

2 oranges, sliced thin

1 lime, sliced thin

1 cup strawberries, sliced

2 Granny Smith apples, cored and diced

¼ cup brandy

1 cup lemon seltzer

1. Place all of the ingredients, except for the seltzer, in a large pitcher and stir to combine. Cover with plastic wrap and chill the mixture in the refrigerator for 4 or more hours.

2. When ready to serve, add ice and seltzer, gently stir, and enjoy.

GLASSWARE: Pint glasses
GARNISH: Chamoy, splash of lime juice, lime wheel, and Tajín

---

2 cups clamato

¼ cup green olive brine

1 tablespoon Tajín

1 tablespoon soy sauce

1 tablespoon Maggi seasoning sauce

1 tablespoon celery salt

¼ cup fresh lime juice

1 teaspoon Tabasco

2 teaspoons Worcestershire sauce

Salt and pepper, to taste

12 oz. Mexican lager

1 oz. chamoy, for garnish

---

1. Place all of the ingredients in a mixing bowl and stir to combine. Refrigerate the mixture overnight.

2. If desired, rim the pint glasses with salt. Fill them halfway with the michelada mix, pour the beer on top, and gently stir to combine. Garnish with chamoy, lime juice, lime wheel, and Tajín and enjoy.

MICHELADA

CORPSE REVIVER #2

GLASSWARE: Cocktail glass
GARNISH: Citrus twist

---

1 oz. London dry gin
1 oz. Cointreau
1 oz. Lillet
1 oz. fresh lemon juice
Dash of absinthe

---

1. Place all of the ingredients in a cocktail shaker, fill it two-thirds of the way with ice, and shake until chilled.

2. Strain into the cocktail glass, garnish with the citrus twist, and enjoy.

RAMOS GIN FIZZ

GLASSWARE: Collins glass
GARNISH: Lemon slice (optional)

---

2 oz. gin
1 oz. half & half
¾ oz. Simple Syrup (see page 35)
½ oz. fresh lemon juice
½ oz. fresh lime juice
2 dashes of orange blossom water
1 egg white
Club soda, to top

---

1. Chill the Collins glass in the refrigerator.

2. Place all of the ingredients, except for the club soda, in a cocktail shaker and dry shake for 15 seconds.

3. Fill the shaker one-quarter of the way with ice and shake for 3 minutes.

4. Pour the cocktail into the chilled glass and top with club soda, pouring slowly.

5. Garnish with the lemon slice (if desired) and enjoy.

TIME TO CELEBRATE

Brunch is nothing if not a celebration, an opportunity to give your friends and loved ones something to remember, and to revel in all of the small, good things we are fortunate to have in our lives: free time, good people, great food, and exceptional drinks. The cocktails in this chapter are intended to rise to meet such occasions, providing a mix of sparkling serves that automatically make things feel more festive, and tropically inclined drinks that signal to everyone that the party has begun. If you're in the mood for one of those brunches that stretches out into an all-day hang, start your menu planning here.

GLASSWARE: Collins glass
GARNISH: None

2 oz. gin

¾ oz. fresh lemon juice

½ oz. crème de violette

¼ oz. Orgeat (see page 70)

¼ oz. Rich Simple Syrup (see recipe)

½ oz. egg white

¼ oz. Passion Fruit Syrup (see recipe)

¼ oz. blue curaçao

1 oz. sparkling water, chilled, to top

1. Place all of the ingredients, except for the sparkling water, in a cocktail shaker and dry shake for 10 seconds.

2. Add ice and shake vigorously until chilled.

3. Double strain over 2 ice cubes into the Collins glass, top with the sparkling water, and enjoy.

RICH SIMPLE SYRUP: Place 2 cups sugar and 1 cup water in a saucepan and bring it to a boil, stirring to dissolve the sugar. Remove the pan from heat and let the syrup cool completely before using or storing.

PASSION FRUIT SYRUP: Place 1½ cups passion fruit puree and 1½ cups Demerara Syrup (see page 103) in a mason jar, seal it, and shake until combined. Use immediately or store in the refrigerator.

VIOLET FIZZ

PORT IN A STORM

GLASSWARE: Collins glass
GARNISH: Peychaud's Bitters, freshly grated nutmeg, fresh mint, grapefruit twist

---

1¼ oz. Damrak Gin
½ oz. Bénédictine
¼ oz. almond liqueur
1 bar spoon of St. Elizabeth Allspice Dram
½ oz. Ginger Syrup (see recipe)
½ oz. passion fruit puree
½ oz. fresh lime juice
¾ oz. grapefruit juice

---

1. Place all of the ingredients in a cocktail shaker, fill it two-thirds of the way with ice, and shake until chilled.

2. Strain over ice into the Collins glass, garnish with bitters, nutmeg, fresh mint, and the grapefruit twist, and enjoy.

GINGER SYRUP: Place 1 cup water and 1 cup sugar in a saucepan and bring the mixture to a boil, stirring to dissolve the sugar. Add a peeled 1-inch piece of fresh ginger, remove the pan from heat, and let the syrup cool completely. Strain before using or storing.

GLASSWARE: Rocks glass
GARNISH: Strip of orange peel

---

2 oz. Cocoa Puff–Infused Bourbon (see recipe)
5 drops of white soy sauce
2 dashes of Bittermens Xocolatl Mole Bitters
¼ oz. Simple Syrup (see page 35)

---

1. Place all of the ingredients in a mixing glass, fill it two-thirds of the way with ice, and stir until chilled.

2. Strain over a large ice cube into the rocks glass, garnish with the strip of orange peel, and enjoy.

COCOA PUFF–INFUSED BOURBON:

Place 1 box of Cocoa Puffs and a 750 ml bottle of bourbon in a large container and let the mixture steep for 1 day. Strain before using or storing.

CUCKOO FOR COCOA PUFFS

THE ESCAPE

GLASSWARE: Brandy snifter
GARNISH: Pineapple chunk, maraschino cherry

---

2 oz. aged rum (Demerara preferred)

1 oz. pineapple juice

1 oz. cream of coconut

¾ oz. sweet vermouth, to float

1. Place the rum, pineapple juice, and cream of coconut in a cocktail shaker, fill it two-thirds of the way with ice, and shake until chilled.

2. Fill the brandy snifter with crushed ice and strain the cocktail over it.

3. Float the vermouth on top of the cocktail, pouring it over the back of a bar spoon.

4. Garnish with the pineapple chunk and maraschino cherry and enjoy.

FORMOSA FIZZ

GLASSWARE: Champagne flute
GARNISH: Fresh raspberries

1½ oz. silver tequila

¾ oz. fresh lemon juice

½ oz. Raspberry Syrup (see recipe)

½ oz. egg white

¼ oz. Rich Simple Syrup (see page 49)

1½ oz. soda water, chilled

1. Place all of the ingredients, except for the soda water, in a cocktail shaker, fill it two-thirds of the way with ice, and shake until chilled and foamy.

2. Strain into the Champagne flute and top with the soda water.

3. Garnish with fresh raspberries and enjoy.

RASPBERRY SYRUP: Combine 500 grams raspberries and 500 grams sugar in a deep saucepan, then gently press down the mixture with the back of a fork. Let it macerate for 15 minutes, then add 500 ml water. Bring the mixture to just below a boil. Remove the pan from heat and let the syrup cool for 30 minutes. Strain the syrup through a fine-mesh sieve or cheesecloth before using or storing in the refrigerator.

PACIFIC RHYTHMS

GLASSWARE: Collins glass
GARNISH: Fresh mint, lime wheel, edible flower

Matcha powder, for the rim

Sugar, for the rim

2 cucumber slices

2 oz. Beluga Noble Vodka

½ oz. Midori

½ oz. Luxardo maraschino liqueur

¾ oz. fresh lemon juice

½ oz. Simple Syrup (see page 35)

Fever-Tree Sparkling Lime & Yuzu, to top

---

1. Combine matcha powder and sugar in a small dish. Wet the rim of the Collins glass and coat it with mixture. Add ice to the rimmed glass.

2. Place all of the remaining ingredients, except the tonic water, in a cocktail shaker and muddle.

3. Add ice and shake until chilled.

4. Strain the cocktail into the rimmed glass and top with tonic water.

5. Garnish with fresh mint, a lime wheel, and an edible flower and enjoy.

GO AHEAD, ROMEO

GLASSWARE: Brandy snifter
GARNISH: Orange twist

---

6 Aperol Ice Cubes (see recipe)

4 oz. prosecco

1. Place the Aperol Ice Cubes in the snifter and pour the prosecco over them.

2. Garnish with the orange twist and enjoy.

APEROL ICE CUBES: Combine ¼ cup Aperol and ¾ cup water, pour the mixture into ice cube trays, and freeze until solid.

THE ROBIN'S NEST

GLASSWARE: Hurricane glass
GARNISH: Candied pineapple, pineapple leaves

---

1 oz. Suntory Toki Japanese Whisky
½ oz. Plantation O.F.T.D. Rum
½ oz. Cinnamon Syrup (see recipe)
½ oz. fresh lemon juice
¾ oz. pineapple juice
1 oz. Passion Fruit Honey (see recipe)
1 oz. cranberry juice

---

1. Place all of the ingredients, except for the cranberry juice, in a cocktail shaker, fill it two-thirds of the way with ice, and shake vigorously until chilled.

2. Fill the Hurricane glass with crushed ice, strain the cocktail over it, and top with the cranberry juice.

3. Garnish the cocktail with the candied pineapple and pineapple leaves and enjoy.

CINNAMON SYRUP: Place 1 cup water and 2 cinnamon sticks in a saucepan and bring the mixture to a boil. Add 2 cups sugar and stir until it has dissolved. Remove the pan from heat, cover it, and let the mixture steep at room temperature for 12 hours. Strain the syrup through cheesecloth before using or storing.

PASSION FRUIT HONEY: Place 1 cup honey in a saucepan and warm it over medium heat until it is runny. Pour the honey into a mason jar, stir in 1 cup passion fruit puree, and let the mixture cool before using or storing in the refrigerator.

GLASSWARE: Collins glass
GARNISH: Fresh mint

Handful of fresh mint
¾ oz. Del Maguey Vida Mezcal
¾ oz. Smith & Cross Rum
1 oz. fresh lime juice
¾ oz. Thai Chile & Basil Syrup (see recipe)
½ oz. falernum
½ oz. orange juice
Peychaud's Bitters, to top

---

1. Place the fresh mint at the bottom of the Collins glass and fill the glass with pebble ice.

2. Fill the glass with the remaining ingredients, except for the bitters, and top with more pebble ice.

3. Top with bitters until you see a nice red layer on the top of the drink. Garnish with additional fresh mint and enjoy.

THAI CHILE & BASIL SYRUP: Add ⅓ oz. diced Thai chile pepper and a handful of fresh Thai basil to 2 cups of Simple Syrup (see page 35). Let the mixture steep in the refrigerator for 2 days and strain before using or storing.

BOTTLE ROCKET

THE ISLAND IS CALLING

GLASSWARE: Tiki mug
GARNISH: Edible orchid blossom

---

2 oz. black blended rum (such as Coruba, Goslings, or Hamilton 86)

1 oz. bourbon

¼ oz. Bittermens New Orleans Coffee Liqueur

1 oz. fresh lime juice

½ oz. Cinnamon Syrup (see page 60)

½ oz. Honey Syrup (see recipe)

¼ oz. Vanilla Syrup (see page 73)

2 oz. seltzer

---

1. Place all of the ingredients in a cocktail shaker, add crushed ice and 4 to 6 small cubes, and flash mix with a hand blender.

2. Pour the contents of the shaker into the tiki mug.

3. Garnish with the edible orchid blossom and enjoy.

HONEY SYRUP: Place 1½ cups water in a saucepan and bring it to a boil. Add 1½ cups honey and cook until it is just runny. Remove the pan from heat and let the syrup cool before using or storing in the refrigerator.

THE OTHER SIDE OF SUNNY

GLASSWARE: Collins glass
GARNISH: 3 pineapple leaves, edible orchid

---

1 oz. Plantation 3 Stars Rum

½ oz. gin

¾ oz. fresh lemon juice

1 oz. pineapple juice

1 oz. guava puree

¾ oz. Ginger Syrup (see page 50)

1 bar spoon Herbsaint

4 dashes of Angostura Bitters

---

1. Place all of the ingredients, except for the bitters, in a mixing glass, add 2 oz. crushed ice, and stir until foamy.

2. Pour the contents of the mixing glass into the Collins glass, add the bitters, and top with more crushed ice.

3. Garnish with the pineapple leaves and edible orchid and enjoy.

GLASSWARE: Tumbler
GARNISH: Fresh Thai basil

1½ oz. lightly aged rum

¾ oz. Mango & Oolong Syrup (see recipe)

¾ oz. fresh lime juice

¼ oz. Orgeat (see page 70)

¼ oz. falernum

10 drops of 10 Percent Saline Solution
(see page 141)

Dash of absinthe

---

1. Place all of the ingredients in a cocktail shaker, fill it two-thirds of the way with ice, and shake until chilled.

2. Fill the tumbler with crushed ice and strain the cocktail over it.

3. Top with more crushed ice, garnish with the fresh Thai basil, and enjoy.

MANGO & OOLONG SYRUP: Place ¾ cup water in a saucepan and heat it to 195°F. Add ¼ cup loose-leaf oolong tea and steep for 5 minutes. Strain the tea, discard the leaves, and return the tea to the saucepan. Add 30 oz. mango puree, 30 oz. sugar, 1 (12 oz.) can of mango nectar, and a scant 2½ teaspoons citric acid and warm the mixture over low heat, stirring to dissolve the sugar. When the syrup is well combined, remove the pan from heat and let it cool completely before using or storing.

SECRET LIFE OF PLANTS

RUM BA BA

GLASSWARE: Rocks glass
GARNISH: Passion fruit slice, fresh mint

1½ oz. Appleton Estate Reserve Blend Rum

1½ oz. heavy cream

1 oz. Orgeat (see recipe)

½ oz. fresh lemon juice

1¼ oz. passion fruit puree

2 dashes of Peychaud's Bitters

---

1. Place all of the ingredients in a cocktail shaker, fill it two-thirds of the way with ice, and shake until chilled.

2. Fill a rocks glass with ice and double strain the cocktail over it.

3. Garnish with the passion fruit slice and fresh mint and enjoy.

ORGEAT: Preheat the oven to 400°F. Place 2 cups almonds on a baking sheet, place them in the oven, and toast until they are fragrant, about 5 minutes. Remove the almonds from the oven and let them cool completely. Place the almonds in a food processor and pulse until they are a coarse meal. Set the almonds aside. Place 1 cup Demerara Syrup (see page 103) in a saucepan and warm it over medium heat. Add the almond meal, remove the pan from heat, and let the mixture steep for 6 hours. Strain the mixture through cheesecloth and discard the solids. Stir in 1 teaspoon orange blossom water and 2 oz. vodka and use immediately or store in the refrigerator.

A LA SALA

GLASSWARE: Double rocks glass
GARNISH: Pineapple leaf, edible orchid

1½ oz. Coruba Dark Rum

½ oz. Wray & Nephew Overproof Rum

¾ oz. fresh lime juice

½ oz. pineapple juice

½ oz. cold-brew coffee

½ oz. Ginger Syrup (see page 50)

¾ oz. Vanilla Syrup (see recipe)

1. Place all of the ingredients in a cocktail shaker, fill it halfway with crushed ice, and shake until chilled.

2. Pour the contents of the shaker into the double rocks glass, garnish with the pineapple leaf and edible orchid, and enjoy.

VANILLA SYRUP: Place 1 cup water in a small saucepan and bring it to a boil. Add 2 cups sugar and stir until it has dissolved. Remove the pan from heat. Halve 1 vanilla bean and scrape the seeds into the syrup. Cut the vanilla bean pod into thirds and add the pieces to the syrup. Stir to combine, cover the pan, and let the mixture sit at room temperature for 12 hours. Strain the syrup through cheesecloth before using or storing.

RICERCAR

GLASSWARE: Small clay pot
GARNISH: Lime wheel, cinnamon stick, fresh mint

1½ oz. tequila
1 oz. Ancho Reyes
2½ oz. Pear & Cardamom Horchata (see recipe)
½ oz. fresh lime juice
Dash of Angostura Bitters

---

1. Place all of the ingredients in a cocktail shaker, fill it two-thirds of the way with ice, and shake vigorously until chilled.

2. Fill the clay pot with crushed ice and double strain the cocktail over it.

3. Garnish the cocktail with the lime wheel, cinnamon stick, and fresh mint and enjoy.

PEAR & CARDAMOM HORCHATA: Preheat the oven to 350°F. Place 3½ cinnamon sticks, 14 green cardamom pods, and ¾ of a nutmeg seed on a baking sheet, place it in the oven, and toast the spices for 20 minutes. Remove them from the oven and let them cool. Place 7 cups pear juice, 4 cups water, 4¼ cups jasmine rice, 2 cups honey, 1 vanilla bean, zest of 1 lime, and the toasted aromatics in a large container and let the mixture steep at room temperature overnight. Working in batches, place the mixture in a food processor and blitz until smooth. Double strain the mixture, pressing down on the solids to extract as much liquid as possible. For every 4 cups of horchata, stir in 2 oz. of Cinnamon Syrup (see page 60). Use immediately or store in the refrigerator, where it will keep for up to 1 week.

GLASSWARE: Shot glasses
GARNISH: None

1½ oz. Plantation Stiggins Fancy Pineapple Rum
½ oz. Giffard Abricot du Roussillon
1 oz. pineapple juice
½ oz. fresh lime juice
¼ oz. Simple Syrup (see page 35)
4 dashes of Peychaud's Bitters, to top

---

1. Place all of the ingredients, except for the bitters, in a cocktail shaker, fill it two-thirds of the way with ice, and shake until chilled.

2. Double strain into 2 shot glasses, top each shot with the bitters, and enjoy.

NOTHING'S WRONG

RITZ SPRITZ

GLASSWARE: Coupe
GARNISH: Orange twist

¾ oz. Cognac

½ oz. curaçao

¼ oz. Luxardo maraschino liqueur

¼ oz. fresh lemon juice

Champagne, chilled, to top

1. Chill the coupe in the freezer.

2. Place the Cognac, curaçao, and Luxardo in a mixing glass, fill it two-thirds of the way with ice, and stir until chilled.

3. Strain into the chilled coupe and top with Champagne.

4. Garnish with the orange twist and enjoy.

GLASSWARE: Wineglass
GARNISH: None

---

1 sprig of fresh rosemary
1 strip of grapefruit peel
1½ oz. elderflower liqueur, chilled
Prosecco, chilled, to top

---

1. Chill the wineglass in the freezer.

2. Rub the rosemary and strip of grapefruit peel around the inside of the wineglass and set them aside.

3. Pour the liqueur into the glass and top with the prosecco.

4. Gently add ice to the cocktail, place the rosemary and strip of grapefruit peel on top, and enjoy.

ELDERFLOWER SPRITZ

LITTLE GREEN APPLES

Maple sugar, for the rim
Salt, for the rim
1¼ oz. Casamigos Añejo Tequila
¼ oz. fresh lime juice
1 oz. freshly pressed cucumber juice
2 oz. freshly pressed apple juice

1. Combine maple sugar and salt in a dish and rim the Collins glass with the mixture. Fill the glass with ice.

2. Place the remaining ingredients in a cocktail shaker, fill it two-thirds of the way with ice, and shake until chilled.

3. Strain the cocktail into the rimmed glass and enjoy.

GLASSWARE: Wineglass
GARNISH: Orange twist

1½ oz. Aperol
Prosecco, to top
Splash of cranberry juice
2 fresh mint leaves

---

1. Fill the wineglass with ice and add the Aperol.

2. Top with prosecco and add the cranberry juice and fresh mint.

3. Garnish with the orange twist and enjoy.

I'M THE QUEEN

VACATION FROM MY MIND

¾ oz. mezcal

½ oz. cachaça

½ oz. Toasted Black Cardamom & Cinnamon Maple Syrup (see recipe)

½ oz. fresh lime juice

¼ oz. pisco

¼ oz. apricot liqueur

¼ oz. Ancho Reyes

½ oz. Orgeat (see page 70)

¼ oz. falernum

2 dashes of Bittermens Xocolatl Mole Bitters

Pinch of salt

1. Place all of the ingredients in a cocktail shaker, fill it two-thirds of the way with ice, and shake until chilled.

2. Fill the rocks glass with crushed ice and strain the cocktail over it.

3. Garnish with crushed cinnamon sticks and enjoy.

TOASTED BLACK CARDAMOM & CINNAMON MAPLE SYRUP: Place 2 cinnamon sticks and 3 black cardamom pods in a skillet and toast over medium heat until fragrant, shaking the pan frequently. Remove the aromatics from the pan and set them aside. Place 1 cup maple syrup and ½ cup water in a saucepan and bring to a simmer. Add the toasted spices and simmer for 5 minutes. Remove the pan from heat and let the mixture cool for 1 hour. Strain before using or storing.

GLASSWARE: Collins glass
GARNISH: Fresh mint, lemon twist

---

2 oz. Mint Bourbon (see recipe)

2 oz. Watermelon Juice (see recipe)

1 oz. fresh lemon juice

1 oz. Honey Syrup (see page 64)

3 dashes of Peychaud's Bitters

---

1. Place all of the ingredients in a cocktail shaker, fill it two-thirds of the way with ice, and shake until chilled.

2. Strain the cocktail over ice into the Collins glass, garnish with fresh mint and the lemon twist, and enjoy.

MINT BOURBON: Place 1 liter of bourbon and 2 large handfuls of fresh mint in a large container and steep for 24 hours. Strain before using or storing.

WATERMELON JUICE: Puree watermelon chunks in a blender, strain through a fine-mesh sieve, and use immediately or store in the refrigerator.

SUMMER BREEZE

COTTAGE BY THE SEASIDE

GLASSWARE: Coupe
GARNISH: Pineapple leaf

2 oz. fresh pineapple juice

1 oz. reposado tequila

1 oz. Jamaican rum

1 oz. fresh grapefruit juice

Dash of Green Tabasco, or to taste

1. Place all of the ingredients in a cocktail shaker, fill it two-thirds of the way with ice, and shake until chilled.

2. Strain into the coupe, garnish with the pineapple leaf, and enjoy.

GLASSWARE: Champagne flute
GARNISH: None

1½ oz. Effen Blood Orange Vodka

¾ oz. Aperol

1 oz. fresh lemon juice

½ oz. Simple Syrup (see page 35)

½ oz. egg white

1 oz. prosecco, plus more to top

---

1. Chill the Champagne flute in the freezer.

2. Place all of the ingredients, except for the prosecco, in a cocktail shaker containing 1 large ice cube and shake until chilled.

3. Pour the prosecco into the chilled Champagne flute and strain the cocktail over it.

4. Top with additional prosecco and enjoy.

BRIGHTER DAYS

VISIONS OF DAWN

GLASSWARE: Collins glass
GARNISH: Pineapple wedge, pineapple leaf

1½ oz. reposado tequila
½ oz. pineapple rum
¼ oz. Licor 43
2 oz. pineapple juice
1 oz. orange juice
1 oz. coconut horchata
2 dashes of Angostura Bitters
Blue curaçao, to top

---

1. Place all of the ingredients, except for the curaçao, in a cocktail shaker, fill it two-thirds of the way with ice, and shake until chilled.

2. Strain the cocktail over ice into the Collins class and top with curaçao.

3. Garnish with the pineapple wedge and pineapple leaf and enjoy.

GLASSWARE: Coupe
GARNISH: Edible flower blossoms or fresh raspberry

---

3 to 4 fresh raspberries
1½ oz. vodka or gin
½ oz. Simple Syrup (see page 35)
½ oz. fresh lemon juice
1½ oz. Champagne or sparkling rosé

---

1. Chill the coupe in the freezer.

2. Place all of the ingredients, except for the Champagne, in a cocktail shaker, fill it two-thirds of the way with ice, and shake until chilled.

3. Double strain the cocktail into the chilled coupe.

4. Top with the Champagne, garnish with edible flower blossoms or a raspberry, and enjoy.

BERRIES & BUBBLES

STYLISH
SERVES

Though brunch is overwhelmingly inclined more toward cultivating enjoyment than urging proper conduct, there will inevitably be a few occasions where you want to strike a more refined air with a brunch. Perhaps it is a particular menu item you've been wanting to try. Perhaps you found a lovely arrangement down at the flower shop and are following its lead. Or perhaps you just feel like being a little bit fancy. Whatever it is, these elegant cocktails will help you strike the proper tone, setting the stage for a brunch that beautifully walks the thin line between sophistication and fun.

GLASSWARE: Coupe
GARNISH: Chamomile blossoms, ground freeze-dried raspberries

1½ oz. gin
¼ oz. absinthe
¾ oz. Chamomile Syrup (see recipe)
1 oz. coconut milk
½ oz. aquafaba

---

1. Place all of the ingredients in a cocktail shaker, fill it two-thirds of the way with ice, and shake until chilled.

2. Strain the cocktail into the coupe, garnish with chamomile blossoms and ground freeze-dried raspberries, and enjoy.

CHAMOMILE SYRUP: Add 1 tablespoon of chamomile blossoms or 2 bags of chamomile tea to the Simple Syrup (see page 35) after the sugar has dissolved. Let the syrup cool and strain before using or storing in the refrigerator.

WHITECAPS

CAFFE NEGRONI

GLASSWARE: Rocks glass
GARNISH: Strip of orange peel

---

1 oz. The Botanist Islay Dry Gin
½ oz. Espresso-Infused Campari (see recipe)
½ oz. sweet vermouth
¾ oz. Mr Black Coffee Liqueur
Dash of Fee Brothers Aztec Chocolate Bitters

---

1. Place all of the ingredients in a cocktail shaker, fill it two-thirds of the way with ice, and shake until chilled.

2. Strain over ice into the rocks glass, garnish with the strip of orange peel, and enjoy.

ESPRESSO-INFUSED CAMPARI: Place 2 tablespoons espresso beans and a 750 ml bottle of Campari in a large mason jar and let the mixture steep for 3 hours. Strain before using or storing.

GLASSWARE: Cocktail glass
GARNISH: Edible flower blossoms

---

5 pineapple chunks

1½ oz. Knob Creek Bourbon

1 oz. Amaro Nonino

3 dashes of Angostura Bitters

½ oz. Demerara Syrup (see recipe)

½ oz. fresh lemon juice

½ oz. pineapple juice

¾ oz. sparkling wine

ANANDA SPRITZ

1. Place the pineapple in a cocktail shaker and muddle it.

2. Add all of the remaining ingredients, except for the sparkling wine, fill the shaker two-thirds of the way with ice, and shake until chilled.

3. Strain the cocktail into the cocktail glass and top with the sparkling wine.

4. Garnish with edible flower blossoms and enjoy.

DEMERARA SYRUP: Place 1 cup water in a saucepan and bring it to a boil. Add ½ cup demerara sugar and 1½ cups sugar and stir until they have dissolved. Remove the pan from heat and let the syrup cool completely before using or storing.

GLEAMING THE CUBE

GLASSWARE: Rocks glass
GARNISH: Orange wedge

---

2 oz. Tapatio Tequila
½ oz. Pierre Ferrand Dry Curaçao
1 oz. fresh lime juice
¼ oz. agave nectar

1. Place all of the ingredients in a cocktail shaker, fill it two-thirds of the way with ice, and shake vigorously until chilled.

2. Double strain over a Hibiscus Ice Cube (see recipe) into the rocks glass, garnish with the orange wedge, and enjoy.

HIBISCUS ICE CUBES: Place 8 cups water, 1 cup dried hibiscus blossoms, and an entire orange peel in a saucepan and bring to a boil. Remove the pan from heat and let the mixture steep for 3 hours. Strain, pour the strained liquid into ice molds, and freeze.

HOME IS WHERE THE HEAT IS

GLASSWARE: Double rocks glass
GARNISH: Dehydrated jalapeño slice

Lava salt, for the rim

Cumin, for the rim

1½ oz. Spicy Mezcal (see recipe)

¼ oz. Giffard Banane du Brésil

½ oz. fresh lime juice

½ oz. Manzanilla sherry

¾ oz. Tamarind Syrup (see recipe)

---

1. Place lava salt and cumin in a dish and stir to combine. Wet the rim of the double rocks glass and coat it with the mixture.

2. Place the remaining ingredients in a cocktail shaker, fill it two-thirds of the way with ice, and shake until chilled.

3. Strain over ice into the rimmed glass, garnish with the dehydrated slice of jalapeño, and enjoy.

SPICY MEZCAL: Place sliced jalapeño in a bottle of mezcal and let it steep for 24 hours—determine the amount of jalapeños and the length of time you steep the mixture based on your spice tolerance. Strain before using or storing, and reserve the leftover jalapeños to garnish other cocktails or serve as a boozy and yummy snack.

TAMARIND SYRUP: Place ¼ cup tamarind pulp, 1 cup water, and 1 cup sugar in a saucepan and bring to a simmer, stirring to dissolve the sugar and incorporate the tamarind. Remove the pan from heat and let the mixture cool completely. Strain before using or storing.

GLASSWARE: Coupe
GARNISH: Dehydrated lime slice

Citrus Salt (see recipe), for the rim

2 oz. Avión Silver Tequila

2 oz. Avocado Mix (see recipe)

¾ oz. fresh lime juice

½ oz. agave nectar

1 egg white

---

1. Wet the rim of the coupe and dip it into the Citrus Salt.

2. Place all of the remaining ingredients in a cocktail shaker, fill it two-thirds of the way with ice, and shake until chilled.

3. Strain the cocktail into the coupe, garnish with the dehydrated lime slice, and enjoy.

CITRUS SALT: Place ½ cup salt, the zest of 2 lemons, and the zest of 2 limes in an airtight container and stir to combine. Use immediately or store at room temperature.

AVOCADO MIX: Place the flesh of 3 avocados, 2 lbs. peeled and cored pineapple, and ¾ lb. cilantro in a blender and puree until smooth. Use immediately or store in the refrigerator.

THE FIFTH ELEMENT

APPLELIZA

GLASSWARE: Collins glass
GARNISH: Cucumber ribbon

1⅓ oz. Del Maguey Vida Mezcal

⅓ oz. fresh lime juice

2⅓ oz. apple juice

⅔ oz. Amaro Montenegro

⅓ oz. Cucumber Cordial (see recipe)

---

1. Chill the Collins glass in the freezer.

2. Fill the chilled glass with ice, add all of the ingredients, and gently stir until chilled.

3. Garnish with the cucumber ribbon and enjoy.

CUCUMBER CORDIAL: Place 1 cucumber peel, ¼ teaspoon Maldon sea salt, 1 cup caster (superfine) sugar, and 2 cups water in a blender and puree until smooth. Strain before using or storing in the refrigerator.

GLASSWARE: Coupe
GARNISH: Maraschino cherry

---

1 oz. tequila

⅔ oz. Aperol

½ oz. Giffard Rhubarb Liqueur

⅓ oz. dry vermouth

1 oz. iced peach tea

---

1. Chill the coupe in the freezer.

2. Place all of the ingredients in a mixing glass, fill it two-thirds of the way with ice, and stir until chilled.

3. Strain into the chilled coupe, garnish with the maraschino cherry, and enjoy.

RED RHUBY

THE PROJECT

GLASSWARE: Rocks glass
GARNISH: Torched strip of orange peel, coffee beans

---

2 oz. Santa Teresa 1796 Rum

¼ oz. Cynar

1 oz. Aperol

¼ oz. Coffee Syrup (see recipe)

1. Place all of the ingredients in a cocktail shaker, fill it two-thirds of the way with ice, and shake until chilled.

2. Double strain over an ice sphere into the rocks glass, garnish with the torched orange peel and coffee beans, and enjoy.

COFFEE SYRUP: Place equal parts water and sugar in a saucepan and add coffee beans, using 10 beans per quart of water. Bring to a boil, remove the pan from heat, and the mixture steep for 4 hours. Strain before using or storing in the refrigerator.

GLASSWARE: Collins glass
GARNISH: 1 teaspoon shaved fresh ginger, fresh mint

---

2 oz. Appleton Estate Reserve Blend Rum

1 oz. coconut milk

1 oz. fresh lime juice

1 oz. Demerara Syrup (see page 103)

---

1. Place all of the ingredients in a cocktail shaker, fill it two-thirds of the way with ice, and shake until chilled.

2. Fill the Collins glass with crushed ice and strain the cocktail over it.

3. Top with more crushed ice, garnish with the shaved ginger and fresh mint, and enjoy.

THE POWER OF ONE

ROOT HEALER

GLASSWARE: Coupe
GARNISH: None

Smoked salt, for the rim

1½ oz. pear vodka

¼ oz. Calvados VSOP

¼ oz. Asian pear puree

1 oz. tamarind nectar

¼ oz. Passion Fruit Syrup (see page 49)

¼ oz. fresh lime juice

2 fresh shiso leaves

½ oz. Simple Syrup (see page 35)

---

1. Wet the rim of the coupe and coat it with smoked salt.

2. Add all of the remaining ingredients to a cocktail shaker, fill it two-thirds of the way with ice, and shake until chilled.

3. Double strain the cocktail into the coupe and enjoy.

GLASSWARE: Rocks glass
GARNISH: Fried curry leaf

---

2 oz. Smoked Rasam (see recipe)

2 oz. vodka

¾ oz. honey

¾ oz. fresh lime juice

1 oz. club soda

---

1. Place all of the ingredients in a mixing glass, stir to combine, and then carbonate the cocktail.

2. Pour the cocktail over ice into the rocks glass, garnish with the fried curry leaf, and enjoy.

SMOKED RASAM: Dice 15 tomatoes, place them in a saucepan, and cook over medium heat for about 20 minutes. Add coriander seeds, curry leaves, mustard seeds to taste, and the Masala Water (see recipe), stir to combine, and remove the pan from heat. Place the saucepan in a large roasting pan. Place hickory wood chips in a ramekin, coat a strip of paper towel with canola oil, and insert it in the center of the wood chips. Set the ramekin in the roasting pan, carefully light the wick, and wait until the wood chips ignite. Cover the roasting pan with aluminum foil and smoke the rasam for 1 hour.

MASALA WATER: Place 2 oz. dried mango in a bowl of hot water and soak it for 30 minutes. Place the rehydrated mango, 3 oz. cilantro, 3 green chile peppers, ½ teaspoon black pepper, ¼ teaspoon grated fresh ginger, and 2 teaspoons dried mint in a food processor and blitz until the mixture is a smooth paste. Stir the paste into 4 cups water and use as desired.

WHISTLEPODU

EAST OF EDEN

GLASSWARE: Coupe
GARNISH: None

1½ oz. vodka
½ oz. coconut rum
¼ oz. heavy cream
½ oz. egg white
½ oz. fresh lemon juice
½ oz. Simple Syrup (see page 35)
2 dashes of lavender bitters

---

1. Place all of the ingredients in a cocktail shaker, fill it two-thirds of the way with ice, and shake until chilled.

2. Strain into the coupe and enjoy.

GLASSWARE: Coupe
GARNISH: Slice of English cucumber

---

1 lime wedge

Dash of caster (superfine) sugar

2 slices of English cucumber

2 oz. Lovejoy Vodka

½ oz. pear nectar

---

1. Place the lime wedge and sugar in a cocktail shaker and muddle.

2. Add ice and the remaining ingredients and shake until chilled.

3. Strain into the coupe, garnish with additional slice of cucumber, and enjoy.

A PERFECT PEAR

MOTHER MARY

GLASSWARE: Collins glass
GARNISH: Pickled vegetables, Spicy Mignonette (see recipe)

---

6 oz. vodka

12 oz. tomato juice

1 oz. seasoned rice vinegar

1 oz. unseasoned rice vinegar

1 oz. Worcestershire sauce

1 oz. fresh lemon juice

1 oz. extra-hot prepared horseradish

16 dashes Tapatío or Crystal hot sauce

8 dashes of celery bitters

4 pinches of salt

20 cracks of black pepper

---

1. Place all of the ingredients in a pitcher and whisk to combine.

2. Fill 4 glasses with ice and pour the drink into them.

3. Garnish with pickled vegetables and the Spicy Mignonette and enjoy.

SPICY MIGNONETTE: Place 1 minced large shallot, 1 minced large jalapeño chile pepper, and ½ bunch of fresh cilantro, finely chopped, in a bowl and stir until well combined. Just before serving, stir in the juice of 1 lime, ¼ cup seasoned rice vinegar, and ¼ cup unseasoned rice vinegar and serve. Use all of the mignonette the same day it's made.

GLASSWARE: Coupe
GARNISH: Luxardo maraschino cherries

---

8 fresh basil leaves
1 (heaping) teaspoon caster (superfine) sugar
1¼ oz. Square One Botanical Vodka
½ oz. Green Chartreuse
¼ oz. Maurin Quina
¾ oz. fresh lime juice

---

1. Chill the coupe in the freezer.

2. Place the fresh basil and sugar in a cocktail shaker and muddle.

3. Add ice and the remaining ingredients and shake until chilled.

4. Double strain into the chilled coupe, garnish with Luxardo maraschino cherries, and enjoy.

THE GREEN KNIGHT

ELEVATED BRILLIANCE

GLASSWARE: Coupe
GARNISH: 3 Recycled Espresso Beans (see recipe)

¼ oz. fresh lemon juice

¼ oz. Toasted Cacao Nib & Espresso Brew (see recipe)

½ oz. Cardamom & Honey Syrup (see recipe)

1½ oz. Paul John Brilliance Whisky

---

1. Chill the coupe in the freezer.

2. Place all of the ingredients in a cocktail shaker, fill it two-thirds of the way with ice, and shake until chilled.

3. Strain into the chilled coupe, garnish with the Recycled Espresso Beans, and enjoy.

TOASTED CACAO NIB & ESPRESSO BREW: Place ½ teaspoon cacao nibs in a dry skillet and toast over medium heat, shaking the pan frequently, until they start to sweat and become extremely fragrant, about 10 minutes. Place the cacao nibs in a mason jar, add ½ teaspoon finely ground espresso and 2 tablespoons lukewarm water, and let the mixture steep overnight. Strain the mixture through a fine-mesh sieve before using or storing in the refrigerator. Reserve the solids for use in the Recycled Espresso Beans.

CARDAMOM & HONEY SYRUP: Place ½ cup wildflower honey, ¼ cup water, and ½ teaspoon ground cardamom in a saucepan and bring to a simmer over medium-low heat, stirring until the honey has emulsified. Remove the pan from heat and let the syrup cool. Strain the syrup through a fine-mesh sieve before using or storing in the refrigerator.

RECYCLED ESPRESSO BEANS: Place 1 melted chocolate bar and 1½ teaspoons Cacao Nib & Espresso Solids in a mixing bowl and stir to combine. Pour the mixture into a silicone coffee bean mold. If this mold is not available, the mixture can also be spread on a parchment-lined baking sheet to make a kind of bark. Place the beans in the freezer until set, about 10 minutes. Remove the beans from the mold and use immediately or store in the refrigerator.

GLASSWARE: Teacup
GARNISH: Fresh mint

2½ oz. Green Tea–Infused Gin (see recipe)
½ oz. Raspberry Syrup (see page 55)
¼ oz. Yellow Chartreuse

1. Chill the teacup in the freezer.

2. Place all of the all ingredients in a cocktail shaker, fill it two-thirds of the way with ice, and shake until chilled.

3. Strain the cocktail into the chilled teacup, garnish with fresh mint, and enjoy.

GREEN TEA–INFUSED GIN: Place ½ cup Aviation Gin and 1 bag of organic green tea in a mason jar and let the mixture steep until the flavor is bright, about 25 minutes. Remove the tea bag and use immediately or store.

TEATIME ACROSS THE POND

EL NOPAL

GLASSWARE: Coupe
GARNISH: 2 spritzes of mezcal

---

1 oz. rum
¾ oz. Fennel & Cactus Syrup (see recipe)
¾ oz. fresh lemon juice
½ oz. Ancho Reyes Verde

---

1. Place all of the ingredients in a cocktail shaker, fill it two-thirds of the way with ice, and shake until chilled.

2. Strain the cocktail into the coupe, spritz with the mezcal, and enjoy.

FENNEL & CACTUS SYRUP: Add 500 ml Simple Syrup (see page 35), 60 grams cleaned, chopped cactus, and 50 grams fennel stems with the fronds to a blender and blend until smooth. Strain before using or storing in the refrigerator.

GLASSWARE: Collins glass
GARNISH: Fresh herbs

1½ oz. Rye & Tea Infusion (see recipe)

¾ oz. Thai Tea Reduction (see recipe)

½ oz. Meletti Amaro

1½ oz. coconut cream

2 dashes of Bittermens Hopped Grapefruit Bitters

Toasted autumn spices, to top

---

1. Place all of the ingredients, except for the autumn spices, in a cocktail shaker, fill it two-thirds of the way with ice, and shake until chilled.

2. Fill the Collins glass with crushed ice and strain the cocktail over it.

3. Top with the autumn spices, garnish with your preferred fresh herbs, and enjoy.

RYE & TEA INFUSION: Line a pour-over coffee maker with a paper filter and place loose-leaf Thai tea, hazelnuts, autumn spices, and dried cranberry hibiscus blossoms in the filter. Slowly pour rye whiskey and then Meletti over the mixture and use as desired.

THAI TEA REDUCTION: Place 1½ cups sugar and 1 cup water in a saucepan, add 1½ teaspoons loose-leaf Thai tea, and bring to a simmer. Cook until the mixture has reduced, stirring occasionally to dissolve the sugar. Remove the pan from heat and let the reduction cool completely. Strain before using or storing.

PAOMO AMBROSIA

GLASSWARE: Rocks glass
GARNISH: Finely ground white ambrosia tea leaves

1½ oz. cachaça
½ oz. sake
1 oz. Banana Syrup (see recipe)
½ oz. yuzu juice
¼ oz. fresh lemon juice
2 crushed shiso leaves
1 egg white
Club soda, to top

---

1. Place all of the ingredients, except for the club soda, in a cocktail shaker and dry shake for 10 seconds.

2. Add ice, shake until chilled, and double strain the cocktail over ice into the rocks glass.

3. Top with club soda, garnish with the ground tea leaves, and enjoy.

BANANA SYRUP: Place 5 peeled bananas and 4 cups Simple Syrup (see page 35) in a saucepan and bring to a boil. Cook for 5 minutes, reduce the heat to medium-low, and simmer for 15 minutes. Strain the syrup and let it cool completely before using or storing.

GLASSWARE: Collins glass
GARNISH: Lemon twist

---

1 oz. soda water

1½ oz. The Botanist Islay Dry Gin

¾ oz. fresh lemon juice

¾ oz. Ginger Solution (see recipe)

½ oz. Sarsaparilla-Infused Honey Syrup (see recipe)

2 dashes of orange bitters

2 dashes of 10 Percent Saline Solution (see recipe)

---

1. Pour the soda water into the Collins glass.

2. Place the remaining ingredients in a cocktail shaker, fill it two-thirds of the way with ice, and shake until chilled.

3. Strain the cocktail into the glass and add ice.

4. Garnish with the lemon twist and enjoy.

GINGER SOLUTION: Place ½ cup hot water, ½ cup evaporated cane sugar, and ½ cup freshly pressed ginger juice in a mason jar, stir until the sugar has dissolved, and enjoy.

SARSAPARILLA-INFUSED HONEY SYRUP: Place 2 cups local honey, 1 cup hot water, and 1 oz. Indian sarsaparilla in a mason jar and stir to combine. Let the mixture steep for 24 hours. Strain before using or storing in the refrigerator.

10 PERCENT SALINE SOLUTION: Place 1 oz. of salt in a measuring cup. Add warm water until you reach 10 oz. and the salt has dissolved. Let the solution cool before using or storing.

THE BEEHIVE

YOU SAY TOMATO

1¼ oz. tequila

¼ oz. basil eau de vie

1 oz. Tomato Water (see recipe)

½ oz. Pink Peppercorn Syrup (see recipe)

½ oz. fresh lime juice

---

1. Place all of the ingredients in a mixing glass, fill it two-thirds of the way with ice, and stir until chilled.

2. Strain the cocktail over ice into the rocks glass, garnish with the sprig of pink pepper, and enjoy.

TOMATO WATER: Place tomatoes in a blender, puree until smooth, and strain through a coffee filter.

PINK PEPPERCORN SYRUP: Place 3 cups sugar and 2 cups water in a saucepan and bring to a simmer, stirring to dissolve the sugar. Add 2 tablespoons pink peppercorns or 10 pink pepper sprigs to the syrup, simmer for 20 minutes, and strain. Let the syrup cool completely before using or storing.

GLASSWARE: Collins glass
GARNISH: Pickled beets, pickled cucumber spear, other pickled vegetables (if desired), fresh dill

---

1½ oz. aquavit
¾ oz. Demitri's Extra Horseradish Bloody Mary Seasoning
4 oz. tomato juice
Pinch of chopped fresh dill

---

1. Build the cocktail in the Collins glass, adding the ingredients in the order they are listed.

2. Fill the glass with ice and stir until chilled.

3. Garnish with pickled beets, the pickled cucumber spear, other pickled vegetables (if desired), and fresh dill and enjoy.

BLOODY SCANDI

AME SOEUR

GLASSWARE: Cocktail glass
GARNISH: Edible flower blossom

1¼ oz. cold-brew coffee

1 oz. Green Chartreuse

1 oz. coconut milk

¾ oz. Simple Syrup (see page 35)

¾ oz. Amaro dell'Etna

Heavy Vanilla Cream (see recipe), to top

1. Place all of the ingredients, except for the vanilla cream, in a cocktail shaker, fill it two-thirds of the way with ice, and shake until chilled.

2. Double strain the cocktail into the cocktail glass and layer vanilla cream on top, pouring it slowly over the back of a spoon.

3. Garnish with the edible flower blossom and enjoy.

HEAVY VANILLA CREAM: Place 1 cup heavy whipping cream, 1 oz. vanilla bean paste, and ½ cup Simple Syrup (see page 35) in a cocktail shaker and shake vigorously until the cream is very thick. Use immediately or store in the refrigerator.

IN NEED OF A LIFT

There are moments when the world, or the previous night, conspires to bring us low, and wear us down. In fact, it could be argued that the entire conceit of brunch originated from one of these moments, providing the weary with a tonic in the form of hair of the dog and a plate of something comforting. These cocktails—some refreshing, some revitalizing, some downright exhilarating—are here to carry you and yours on those mornings where you are desperately in need of a boost. One or two and some playful conversation, and you will all be back believing that all is right with the world.

GLASSWARE: Rocks glass
Garnish: Dehydrated orange slice, charred; dehydrated lime slice; pineapple leaf

---

Salt, for the rim

Black pepper, freshly cracked, for the rim

2 oz. silver tequila

¼ oz. fresh lemon juice

¼ oz. agave nectar

½ oz. fresh orange juice

1½ oz. Turmeric Juice Blend (see recipe)

---

1. Combine salt and pepper in a dish and rim the rocks glass with it.

2. Place the remaining ingredients in a cocktail shaker, fill it two-thirds of the way with ice, and shake until chilled.

3. Strain the cocktail into the rimmed glass and garnish with the dehydrated orange slice, dehydrated lime slice, and pineapple leaf.

TURMERIC JUICE BLEND: Use a juicer to combine 1 large carrot, 1 red apple, a 1½-inch-thick slice of freshly skinned pineapple, and 6 to 7 (3- to 4-inch) pieces of fresh turmeric. The juice remains fresh for 5 days, and it can be frozen.

WAY BACK HOME

MADAME LEE

GLASSWARE: Rocks glass
GARNISH: None

1½ oz. Pimm's No. 1

¾ oz. fresh lime juice

¾ oz. Simple Syrup (see page 35)

½ oz. Jamaican rum

½ oz. fresh purple carrot juice

1 bar spoon rose water, to float

1. Place all of the ingredients, except for the rose water, in a cocktail shaker, fill it two-thirds of the way with ice, and shake until chilled.

2. Strain the cocktail over ice into the rocks glass. Float the rose water on top of the drink, pouring it over the back of a bar spoon, and enjoy.

HOW SWEET I ROAMED

GLASSWARE: Coupe
GARNISH: Lime wheel

---

1 oz. pisco
½ oz. Midori
1 oz. kiwi puree
1 oz. Sauvignon Blanc
¾ oz. Simple Syrup (see page 35)

---

1. Place all of the ingredients in a cocktail shaker, fill it two-thirds of the way with ice, and shake until chilled.

2. Double strain into the coupe, garnish with the lime wheel, and enjoy.

BLACKER THE BERRY, SWEETER THE JUICE

GLASSWARE: Collins glass
GARNISH: Lime wheel, fresh sage

---

5 blackberries

1½ oz. mezcal

¾ oz. St-Germain

½ oz. Ginger Syrup (see page 50)

2 dashes of Bittermens Hellfire Habanero Shrub

¾ oz. fresh lime juice

½ oz. agave nectar

---

1. Place the blackberries in the Collins glass, muddle, and top with crushed ice.

2. Place the remaining ingredients in a cocktail shaker, fill it two-thirds of the way with ice, and shake until chilled.

3. Strain the cocktail into the Collins glass, garnish with the lime wheel and sage leaves, and enjoy.

AGENT DALE COOPER

GLASSWARE: Nick & Nora glass
GARNISH: Strip of orange peel

---

1 oz. freshly brewed espresso
2 oz. mezcal
½ oz. Cinnamon Syrup (see page 60)

---

1. Place all of the ingredients in a cocktail shaker, fill it two-thirds of the way with ice, and shake until chilled.

2. Strain into the Nick & Nora glass and garnish with the strip of orange peel.

GLASSWARE: Coupe
GARNISH: Chipotle chile powder

1½ oz. tequila

½ oz. fresh lemon juice

½ oz. Cucumber Syrup (see recipe)

½ oz. Pickled Strawberry & Fresno Chile Brine (see recipe)

---

1. Chill the coupe in the freezer.

2. Place all of the ingredients in a cocktail shaker, fill it two-thirds of the way with ice, and shake until chilled.

3. Strain the cocktail into the chilled coupe, garnish with the chipotle chile powder, and enjoy.

CUCUMBER SYRUP: Place 1 cup freshly pressed cucumber juice and 1 cup caster (superfine) sugar in a blender and puree until the sugar has dissolved. Use immediately or store in the refrigerator.

PICKLED STRAWBERRY & FRESNO CHILE BRINE:
Place 1 cup white balsamic vinegar, 1 cup water, 1 teaspoon salt, and ¼ cup sugar in a saucepan and bring to a boil, stirring to dissolve the sugar. Place 10 hulled and quartered strawberries and 2 deseeded, sliced Fresno chiles in a heatproof container. Pour the brine over the strawberries and chiles and let the mixture cool to room temperature. Strain before using or storing in the refrigerator.

YOU CAN WIN

OH, WHAT'S THAT?

GLASSWARE: Coupe
GARNISH: 3 espresso beans

---

2 oz. Argonaut Saloon Strength Brandy
1 oz. brewed espresso
½ oz. Mr Black Coffee Liqueur
½ oz. Simple Syrup (see page 35)

---

1. Place all of the ingredients in a cocktail shaker, fill it two-thirds of the way with ice, and shake until chilled.

2. Double strain into the coupe, garnish with the espresso beans, and enjoy.

GLASSWARE: Cocktail glass
GARNISH: Pomegranate concentrate

---

2 oz. Bacardí Superior Rum

2 oz. aged rum

Flesh from ¼ medium-ripe avocado

½ oz. half-and-half

¼ oz. Lemon-Lime Juice (see recipe)

2 oz. Simple Syrup (see page 35)

---

1. Place all of the ingredients in a blender, add 1½ cups ice, and blend until the mixture is silky smooth with no trace of ice—the consistency of the drink should be similar to heavy cream.

2. Pour the cocktail into the wineglass and gently drizzle the pomegranate concentrate over the top. Place a cocktail straw or toothpick at the top of the zigzag pattern, pull through the center of the pomegranate concentrate to make a series of hearts, and enjoy.

LEMON-LIME JUICE: Place 1 (16 oz.) bottle of Santa Cruz 100% Pure Lime Juice and 1 (16 oz.) bottle of Santa Cruz 100% Pure Lemon Juice in a large container and shake to combine. Use immediately or store in the refrigerator.

AVOCADO DAIQUIRI

LIGHT THE LANTERN

GLASSWARE: Collins glass
GARNISH: Fresh mint, freshly grated nutmeg, strip of orange peel

---

1 oz. Wild Turkey 81 Bourbon

½ oz. Fernet Branca Menta

½ oz. Grand Marnier

1 oz. nitro cold brew

¼ oz. Demerara Syrup (see page 103)

2 dashes of 18.21 Japanese Chili & Lime Bitters

---

1. Place all of the ingredients in a cocktail shaker, fill it two-thirds of the way with ice, and shake until chilled.

2. Strain, discard the ice in the shaker, and return the cocktail to the shaker. Dry shake for 10 seconds.

3. Pour the cocktail over ice into the Collins glass, garnish with fresh mint, freshly grated nutmeg, and the strip of orange peel, and enjoy.

GLASSWARE: Cocktail glass
GARNISH: Fresh carrot frond

1½ oz. Spirit Works Barrel Gin

1 oz. Fresh Carrot Juice Syrup (see recipe)

½ oz. fresh lemon juice

¼ oz. Bordiga Extra Dry Vermouth

2 dashes of oloroso sherry

2 dashes of Caraway Tincture (see recipe)

1. Chill the cocktail glass in the freezer.

2. Place all of the ingredients in a cocktail shaker, fill it two-thirds of the way with ice, and shake for 15 seconds.

3. Double strain the cocktail into the chilled cocktail glass, garnish with the carrot frond, and enjoy.

FRESH CARROT JUICE SYRUP: Place 1 cup freshly pressed carrot juice and ½ cup Simple Syrup (see page 35) in a mason jar, stir to combine, and use as desired.

CARAWAY TINCTURE: Place 2 tablespoons caraway seeds and 4 oz. high-proof neutral grain alcohol in a mason jar and steep for at least 24 hours, shaking periodically. Strain before using or storing.

THE GARDEN

GLASSWARE: Tumbler
GARNISH: Thin slice of beet, edible rose petals

1½ oz. gin

½ oz. Rose Syrup (see recipe)

1 oz. fresh beet juice

½ oz. fresh lemon juice

1½ to 2 oz. Q Spectacular Tonic Water

1. Place all of the ingredients in a cocktail shaker, fill it two-thirds of the way with ice, and shake until chilled.

2. Pour the contents of the shaker into the tumbler, garnish with the slice of beet and rose petals, and enjoy.

ROSE SYRUP: Place 1 cup rose water in a saucepan and bring to a boil. Add 1 cup sugar and stir until it has dissolved. Remove the pan from heat and let the syrup cool completely before using or storing in the refrigerator.

GLASSWARE: Stemless wineglass
GARNISH: Berry Compote (see recipe), long strip of lemon peel

2 oz. bourbon

¾ oz. fresh orange juice

½ oz. fresh lemon juice

½ oz. Demerara Syrup (see page 103)

1 oz. Wild Berry Cordial (see recipe)

1. Place all of the ingredients in a cocktail shaker, fill it two-thirds of the way with ice, and shake until chilled.

2. Double strain into the wineglass, garnish with the Berry Compote and long strip of lemon peel, and enjoy.

WILD BERRY CORDIAL: Place 2 pints blueberries, 1 pint blackberries, 1 pint raspberries, 3 cups brown sugar, and 1 cup bourbon in a saucepan and bring it to a boil. Cook until the berries start to break down, remove the pan from heat, and let the cordial cool completely. Double strain before using or storing.

BERRY COMPOTE: Place 1 cup mixed berries in a mason jar, cover them with Cognac, and let the berries macerate for 8 hours. Strain before using or storing in the refrigerator.

BERRY WHITE

PINK SKY

GLASSWARE: Collins glass
GARNISH: Grapefruit wheel, lime wheel, dehydrated grapefruit chip

1½ oz. tequila

1 oz. grapefruit juice

¾ oz. fresh lime juice

¼ oz. Aperol

¼ oz. St-Germain

¼ oz. Thai Pepper Shrub (see recipe)

Fever-Tree Bitter Lemon Soda, to top

1. Place all of the ingredients, except for the soda, in the Collins glass, add ice, and stir until chilled.

2. Top with soda, garnish with the grapefruit wheel, lime wheel, and dehydrated grapefruit chip, and enjoy.

THAI PEPPER SHRUB: Place 4 chopped Thai chile peppers, ¼ cup cane vinegar, and ¼ cup cane sugar in a saucepan and bring to a boil. Cook for 5 minutes, remove the pan from heat, and let the shrub cool completely. Strain before using or storing.

GLASSWARE: Rocks glass
GARNISH: None

1½ oz. mezcal

½ oz. crème de mûre

¾ oz. Ginger & Serrano Syrup (see recipe)

½ oz. fresh lime juice

3 dashes of Peychaud's Bitters

---

1. Place all of the ingredients in a cocktail shaker, stir to combine, fill the shaker two-thirds of the way with ice, and shake vigorously until chilled.

2. Fill the rocks glass with crushed or pebble ice, strain the cocktail over it, and enjoy.

GINGER & SERRANO SYRUP: Place 2 cups sugar, 1 cup water, 3 chopped serrano chile peppers, and 2 large chopped pieces of ginger in a saucepan and bring to a simmer, stirring to dissolve the sugar. Cook for 10 minutes and strain the syrup into a mason jar. Let the syrup cool completely before using or storing in the refrigerator.

NO STOPPING US

SAGED BY THE BELL

GLASSWARE: Rocks glass
GARNISH: Fresh sage

---

2 oz. Hornitos Plata Tequila

¾ oz. fresh lime juice

1 oz. Spicy Hibiscus Syrup (see recipe)

3 to 4 fresh sage leaves

2 dashes of Fee Brothers Peach Bitters

---

1. Place all of the ingredients in a cocktail shaker, fill it two-thirds of the way with ice, and shake until chilled.

2. Double strain over a large ice cube into the rocks glass, garnish with fresh sage, and enjoy.

SPICY HIBISCUS SYRUP: Place 2 cups sugar, 1 cup water, ½ cup dried hibiscus blossoms, and ¼ lemon drop chile pepper in a saucepan and bring to a boil, stirring to dissolve the sugar. Remove the pan from heat and let the mixture steep for 8 hours. Strain before using or storing.

HOLD YOUR HEAD UP

GLASSWARE: Rocks glass
GARNISH: Cucumber curl or apple slice

---

1 oz. silver tequila

½ oz. mezcal

½ oz. agave nectar

½ to ¾ oz. fresh lime juice

1 oz. Green Goddess Juice (see recipe)

Tiny pinch of sea salt

---

1. Place all of the ingredients in a cocktail shaker, fill it two-thirds of the way with ice, and shake until chilled.

2. Strain over ice into the rocks glass, garnish with the cucumber curl or apple slice, and enjoy.

GREEN GODDESS JUICE: Using a juicer, juice ½ bunch of green kale, 1 large green apple, 1 cucumber, and 2 celery stalks, extracting as much juice as possible. Use immediately or store in the refrigerator.

RUNNING UP THAT HILL

GLASSWARE: Mason jar
GARNISH: Lime twist, grapefruit slice

1½ oz. silver tequila

¾ oz. Campari

½ oz. fresh lime juice

½ oz. fresh ruby red grapefruit juice

½ oz. Simple Syrup (see page 35)

Topo Chico, to top

---

1. Place all of the ingredients, except for the Topo Chico, in a cocktail shaker, fill it two-thirds of the way with ice, and shake until chilled.

2. Strain the cocktail over ice into the mason jar and top with Top Chico.

3. Garnish with the lime twist and grapefruit slice and enjoy.

PICK UP THE PIECES

GLASSWARE: Coupe
GARNISH: Black pepper

---

2 tablespoons chopped red bell pepper

2 oz. Hendrick's Gin

¾ oz. Aperol

¾ oz. fresh lemon juice

½ oz. Simple Syrup (see page 35)

1. Place the bell pepper in a cocktail shaker and muddle it.

2. Add ice and the remaining ingredients and shake until chilled.

3. Strain into the coupe, garnish with black pepper, and enjoy.

DOT LINE

GLASSWARE: Rocks glass
GARNISH: None

¼ oz. ground Kenyan coffee

1⅓ oz. Bacardí Superior Carta Blanca Rum

⅔ oz. umeshu

1 bar spoon Pedro Ximénez sherry

1 bar spoon St-Germain

Dash of balsamic vinegar

1. Place a coffee dripper over a mixing glass, line the coffee dripper with a filter, and place the coffee in the filter.

2. Pour the rum, umeshu, sherry, and St-Germain over the coffee and let them drip into the glass.

3. Add the balsamic vinegar to the mixing glass, then ice, and stir to incorporate.

4. Strain over an ice sphere into the rocks glass and enjoy.

GLASSWARE: Coupe
GARNISH: Fresh mint

1½ oz. vodka

1 oz. Blackberry Puree (see recipe)

¾ oz. St-Germain

½ oz. fresh lemon juice

---

1. Chill the coupe in the freezer.

2. Place all of the ingredients in a cocktail shaker, fill it two-thirds of the way with ice, and shake until chilled.

3. Strain the cocktail into the chilled coupe, garnish with fresh mint, and enjoy.

BLACKBERRY PUREE: Place ¼ lb. fresh or thawed frozen blackberries, 2 tablespoons caster (superfine) sugar, 2 tablespoons water, and 2 tablespoons fresh lemon juice in a blender and puree until smooth. Strain before using or storing.

STEP INTO A WORLD

GLASSWARE: Rocks glass
GARNISH: Pineapple leaves

1½ oz. Stoli Vodka
½ oz. Cocchi Americano Rosa
1 oz. Ginger Syrup (see page 50)
1 oz. fresh lemon juice
1 oz. strawberry puree
8 fresh mint leaves

---

1. Place all of the ingredients in a cocktail shaker, fill it two-thirds of the way with ice, and shake until chilled.

2. Double strain over ice into the rocks glass, garnish with pineapple leaves, and enjoy.

GLASSWARE: Nick & Nora glass
GARNISH: 3 espresso beans

¾ oz. vodka

1 oz. cold-brew coffee

1 oz. Mr Black Coffee Liqueur

¼ oz. sweetened condensed milk

---

1. Place all of the ingredients in a cocktail shaker, fill it two-thirds of the way with ice, and shake until chilled.

2. Double strain into the Nick & Nora glass, garnish with the espresso beans, and enjoy.

STRANGE BREW

PROPER CUP

GLASSWARE: Footed pilsner glass
GARNISH: Lemon wheel, lime wheel, apple slices, fresh mint

---

2 cucumber ribbons
2 oz. Pimm's No. 1
¾ oz. Hendrick's Gin
Dash of Angostura Bitters
2 dashes of Peychaud's Bitters
½ oz. fresh lemon juice
½ oz. fresh lime juice
1 oz. Apple Syrup (see recipe)
Ginger beer, to top

---

1. Place the cucumber ribbons in the footed pilsner glass.

2. Place all of the remaining ingredients, except for the ginger beer, in a cocktail shaker, fill it two-thirds of the way with ice, and shake vigorously 20 times.

3. Strain into the glass and top with ginger beer.

4. Garnish with the lemon wheel, lime wheel, apple slices, and fresh mint and enjoy.

APPLE SYRUP: Slice an apple and place it in a medium saucepan with 1 cup water, 1 cup sugar, and ½ teaspoon pure vanilla extract. Bring to a boil over medium heat, reduce the heat to medium-low, and simmer for 5 minutes. Remove the pan from heat and let the syrup cool completely. Strain before using or storing.

ZERO HOUR

While we all like the thought of starting the weekend off with a bang, there will no doubt be times where you or a couple of guests want to take it easy. The zero-proof drinks in this chapter are made for these potentially fraught moments, allowing everyone to sip on something delicious and participate in the celebration that is underway.

IF YOU LIKE PIÑA COLADAS

GLASSWARE: Hurricane glass
GARNISH: Pineapple chunk

---

1 oz. cream of coconut
3 oz. pineapple juice
1 oz. Coffee Syrup (see page 114)
1 pineapple chunk, for garnish

---

1. Place all of the ingredients in a blender, add 5 oz. crushed ice, and puree until smooth.

2. Pour the drink into the Hurricane glass, garnish with the pineapple chunk, and enjoy.

PEACHES EN REGALIA

GLASSWARE: Champagne flute
GARNISH: Peach wedge

---

1 oz. peach nectar

3 oz. orange juice

2 dashes of El Guapo Love Potion Bitters

---

1. Place the ingredients in a cocktail shaker, fill it two-thirds of the way with ice, and shake vigorously until chilled.

2. Strain over ice into the Champagne flute, garnish with the peach wedge, and enjoy.

PEACHES EN REGALIA

See page 197

AVE MARIA

Dash of black pepper, plus more for the rim

½ oz. fresh lime wedge

½ oz. olive brine

2 dashes of horseradish

3 drops of Worcestershire sauce

3 dashes of hot sauce

2 dashes of celery salt

6 oz. tomato juice

1. Wet the rim of the tumbler and coat it with black pepper.

2. Add the remaining ingredients to a cocktail shaker, fill it two-thirds of the way with ice, and shake vigorously until chilled.

3. Add ice to the tumbler and strain the cocktail over it.

4. Garnish with whatever your heart desires and enjoy.

BREAKFAST AT WIMBLEDON

GLASSWARE: Collins glass
GARNISH: Cucumber slices, lemon wheel

---

4 fresh mint leaves
2 oz. sparkling lemonade
1 oz. ginger ale
1 oz. cola
½ oz. orange juice
½ oz. fresh lemon juice
2 drops of El Guapo Love Potion Bitters

---

1. Place the mint leaves in the Collins glass and muddle.

2. Add ice and the remaining ingredients and stir to combine.

3. Garnish with the cucumber slices and lemon wheel and enjoy.

BLACKBIRD

GLASSWARE: Rocks glass
GARNISH: Fresh mint

¾ oz. fresh lime juice

¾ oz. fresh lemon juice

1 oz. Cashew Orgeat (see recipe)

5 fresh blackberries

3 oz. Bottlegreen Blackberry, Apple & Sloe Cordial

---

1. Place the juices, orgeat, and blackberries in a cocktail shaker and muddle.

2. Add ice and shake vigorously until chilled.

3. Double strain over crushed ice into the rocks glass and top with the cordial.

4. Garnish with the fresh mint and enjoy.

CASHEW ORGEAT: Place 1 cup cashew milk in a saucepan and bring it to a simmer. Place 2 cups sugar in a large mason jar, pour the warm cashew milk over the sugar, and stir until it has dissolved. Let the mixture cool completely. Stir in 1 teaspoon orange blossom water and use immediately or store in the refrigerator.

GLASSWARE: Collins glass
GARNISH: None

½ cucumber, peeled and diced
½ cup chopped cantaloupe
½ oz. Cucumber Syrup (see page 161)
3 oz. club soda

1. Place the cucumber, cantaloupe, and syrup in a blender, add 3 oz. crushed ice, and puree until smooth.

2. Pour the puree into the Collins glass, add the club soda, gently stir to combine, and enjoy.

CORDILLERA

WHAT'S UP, DOC?

GLASSWARE: Footed pilsner glass
GARNISH: Carrot greens

---

1 oz. black currant juice

½ oz. Bali Spice Syrup (see recipe)

¾ oz. fresh lemon juice

¾ oz. carrot juice

½ oz. orange juice

¼ oz. Ginger Syrup (see page 50)

¼ oz. maple syrup

1. Place all of the ingredients in a cocktail shaker, fill it two-thirds of the way with ice, and shake vigorously until chilled.

2. Strain over crushed ice into the footed pilsner glass, garnish with the carrot greens, and enjoy.

BALI SPICE SYRUP: Break 4 cinnamon sticks into small pieces. Add those pieces to a spice grinder along with 12 whole cloves and 12 star anise pods. Grind until the spices are fine, about 1 minute. Add the ground spices to a saucepan over medium heat and toast until they are aromatic, shaking the pan continually. Add 2 cups Simple Syrup (see page 35), bring to a boil, and then reduce the heat and simmer for 5 minutes. Turn off the heat and let the syrup cool for about 1 hour. Scrape the bottom of the pan to get all of the little seasoning bits and strain the syrup through a mesh strainer or chinois, using a spatula to help push the syrup through. Use immediately or store in the refrigerator.

BAJA LEMONADE

GLASSWARE: Rocks glass
GARNISH: Lemon wheels, fresh rosemary

---

5 oz. lemonade

1 oz. cream of coconut

Splash of agave nectar

1 sprig of fresh rosemary

1. Place the lemonade, cream of coconut, agave, and rosemary in a cocktail shaker, fill it two-thirds of the way with ice, and shake vigorously until chilled.

2. Double strain over ice into the rocks glass, garnish with the lemon wheels and fresh rosemary, and enjoy.

BAJA LEMONADE

QUIVERING IN TIME

GLASSWARE: Tumbler glass
GARNISH: Fresh thyme

---

2 oz. peach nectar

1 oz. iced peach tea

1 oz. Thyme Syrup (see recipe)

½ oz. fresh lemon juice

---

1. Place all of the ingredients in a cocktail shaker, fill it two-thirds of the way with ice, and shake vigorously until chilled.

2. Strain over ice into the tumbler, garnish with fresh thyme and peach wedge, and enjoy.

THYME SYRUP: Place 1 cup water, 1 cup sugar, and 1 small bundle of fresh thyme in a saucepan and bring to a boil, stirring to dissolve the sugar. Remove the pan from heat and let the mixture steep for 1 hour. Strain and let the syrup cool completely before using or storing.

GLASSWARE: Collins glass
GARNISH: Orange wheel

---

2 oz. iced hibiscus raspberry tea
½ oz. Raspberry & Thyme Shrub (see recipe)
½ oz. grapefruit juice
2 dashes of El Guapo Love Potion Bitters

---

1. Place all of the ingredients in a cocktail shaker, fill it two-thirds of the way with ice, and shake vigorously until chilled.

2. Strain over ice into the Collins glass, garnish with the orange wheel, and enjoy.

RASPBERRY & THYME SHRUB: Place ½ cup sugar, ½ cup white wine vinegar, ½ cup raspberries, and 2 tablespoons fresh thyme in a saucepan and bring to a simmer, mashing the raspberries and stirring to dissolve the sugar. Cook for 5 minutes, remove the pan from heat, and strain the shrub into a mason jar. Let it cool completely before using or storing.

OVER THE RAINBOW

DESERT RAIN

GLASSWARE: Collins glass
GARNISH: Watermelon chunk

1½ cups watermelon cubes
½ cucumber, peeled and diced
8 fresh mint leaves, torn
1 oz. fresh lemon juice
½ oz. Agave Syrup (see recipe)
1 oz. iced prickly pear tea
1 oz. aloe vera juice

1. Place the watermelon and cucumber in a blender and puree until smooth.

2. Strain the puree into a cocktail shaker, add ice and the remaining ingredients, and shake vigorously until chilled

3. Strain over crushed ice into the Collins glass, garnish with the watermelon chunk, and enjoy.

AGAVE SYRUP: Place ¾ cup agave nectar and ¼ cup water in a saucepan and bring to a simmer, stirring occasionally. Cook until the syrup has the desired consistency. Remove the pan from heat and let the syrup cool completely before using or storing.

ON A MISTY MORNING

GLASSWARE: Tumbler
GARNISH: None

---

2 slices of jalapeño chile pepper

½ oz. fresh lime juice

1 teaspoon 10 Percent Saline Solution (see page 141)

2¼ teaspoons matcha powder

1 oz. iced ginger tea

1½ oz. iced green tea

½ oz. Simple Syrup (see page 35)

---

1. Place the jalapeño and lime juice in a cocktail shaker and muddle.

2. Add ice and the remaining ingredients and shake vigorously until chilled.

3. Double strain over ice into the tumbler and enjoy.

CORCOVADO

GLASSWARE: Rocks glass
GARNISH: Orange twist

---

2 oz. espresso, room temperature

2 dashes of El Guapo Chicory Pecan Bitters

¼ oz. Rich Simple Syrup (see page 49)

---

1. Place all of the ingredients in a cocktail shaker, fill it two-thirds of the way with ice, and shake vigorously until chilled.

2. Strain over a large ice cube into the rocks glass, garnish with the orange twist, and enjoy.

METRIC CONVERSIONS

WEIGHTS

1 oz. = 28 grams
2 oz. = 57 grams
4 oz. (¼ lb.) = 113 grams
8 oz. (½ lb.) = 227 grams
16 oz. (1 lb.) = 454 grams

VOLUME MEASURES

⅛ teaspoon = 0.6 ml
¼ teaspoon = 1.23 ml
½ teaspoon = 2.5 ml
1 teaspoon = 5 ml
1 tablespoon (3 teaspoons) = ½ fluid oz. = 15 ml
2 tablespoons = 1 fluid oz. = 29.5 ml
¼ cup (4 tablespoons) = 2 fluid oz. = 59 ml
⅓ cup (5⅓ tablespoons) = 2.7 fluid oz. = 80 ml
½ cup (8 tablespoons) = 4 fluid oz. = 120 ml
⅔ cup (10⅔ tablespoons) = 5.4 fluid oz. = 160 ml
¾ cup (12 tablespoons) = 6 fluid oz. = 180 ml
1 cup (16 tablespoons) = 8 fluid oz. = 240 ml

TEMPERATURE EQUIVALENTS

°F	°C	Gas Mark
225	110	¼
250	130	½
275	140	1
300	150	2
325	170	3
350	180	4
375	190	5
400	200	6
425	220	7
450	230	8
475	240	9
500	250	10

LENGTH MEASURES

1/16 inch = 1.6 mm
⅛ inch = 3 mm
¼ inch = 6.35 mm
½ inch = 1.25 cm
¾ inch = 2 cm
1 inch = 2.5 cm

INDEX

ABOUT CIDER MILL PRESS BOOK PUBLISHERS

Good ideas ripen with time. From seed to harvest, Cider Mill Press brings fine reading, information, and entertainment together between the covers of its creatively crafted books. Our Cider Mill bears fruit twice a year, publishing a new crop of titles each spring and fall.

"Where Good Books Are Ready for Press"

501 Nelson Place
Nashville, Tennessee 37214

cidermillpress.com